When ELEANOR ROOSEVELT Learned to Jump a Horse

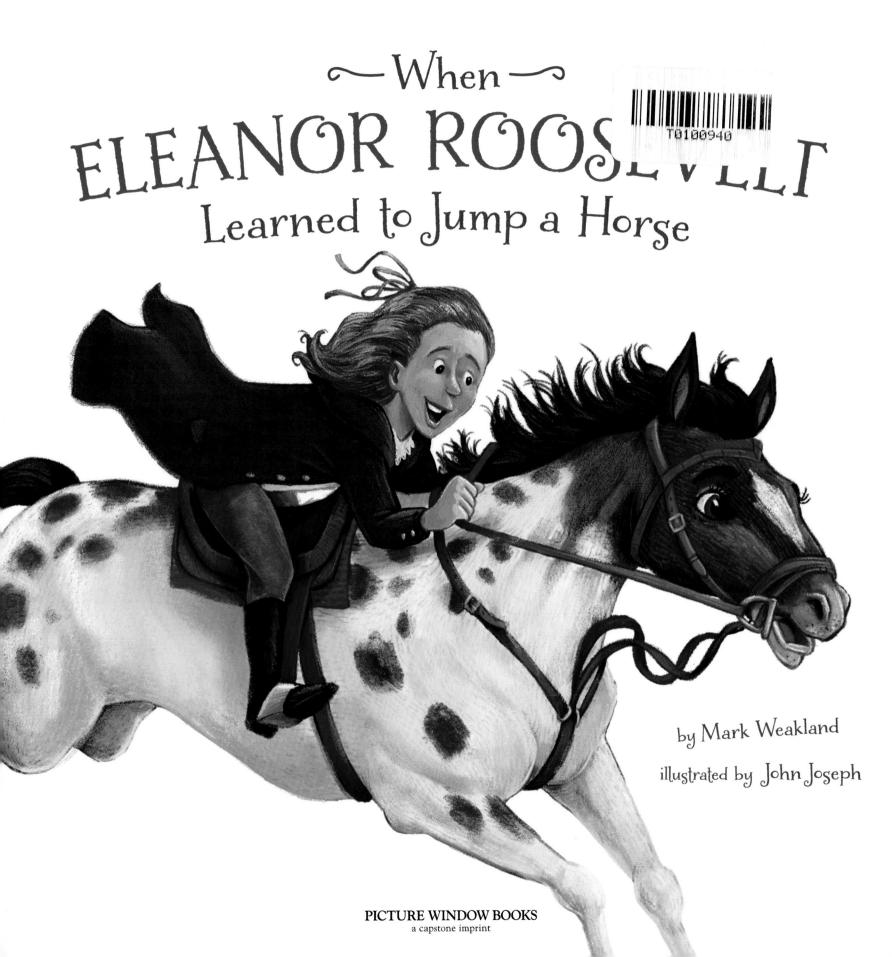

by Mark Weakland

illustrated by John Joseph

PICTURE WINDOW BOOKS
a capstone imprint

Eleanor Roosevelt was one of America's most famous first ladies. She wrote books. She traveled the world. But as a child, she was shy and fearful. Her life was hard. What she wanted most was to love and be loved.

When Eleanor was 7 years old, her mother suffered terrible headaches.

"I can help, Mama," Eleanor said. She sat for hours, gently stroking her mother's head.

Later in life, Eleanor listened as people talked about their struggles. "I can help," she told them. And she did.

Anna Eleanor Roosevelt was born October 11, 1884, in New York City. Her parents were Elliot Roosevelt and Anna Hall. When Eleanor was born, Elliot picked her up. He bounced her in his arms. "You are wrinkly," he said. "But I love you. You are a gift sent from heaven."

Her mother was not as happy. Anna Hall was known for her beauty. She was disappointed by her daughter's looks. "You're such a little granny, so solemn and plain," she said. "Because you have no beauty, you will have to be well behaved."

Eleanor *was* well behaved. But her father was not. He had a hard time focusing. He couldn't hold a job. He was a troubled man. Hoping to help him, Anna took Elliot on a six-month vacation.

Eleanor, who was too young to go, went to stay with relatives. She didn't understand why she had been left behind. **"Where is Baby's home now?"** she asked her aunt.

"Don't be afraid," her aunt replied. "Your parents will be back soon."

Elliot hoped to find a cure for his troubled mind. After four years, Eleanor was allowed to accompany him to health resorts in Europe.

Now Eleanor could be with her father every day. She hiked with him in the woods of Germany. She floated with him on the canals of Venice. Like a real boatman, Elliot sang as he poled through the water.

Eleanor giggled. "I love your voice, Papa," she said. "Sing another song!"

Although Eleanor felt happy at times, she was often afraid. She imagined there were monsters hiding around every corner. But the fear of disappointing her father was real. He was a likeable man, but he had a temper.

During one trip, Elliot took Eleanor into the mountains. He rode a horse. She followed him on a donkey. When they came to a steep hill, Eleanor stopped.

Her father frowned. "You're not afraid, are you?" Eleanor never forgot how harsh his voice sounded.

By the time Eleanor was 7 years old, Elliot was still having some problems. Elliot's older brother was the future 26th U.S. president, Teddy Roosevelt. Teddy told Elliot, "Leave your family for two years. This will give you time to heal."

Elliot followed that advice. But Eleanor had a hard time when her father was away. She didn't understand why he was gone. Elliot would return to visit Eleanor and her two brothers. When Eleanor heard his voice at the front door, she felt joyful. She raced from her room, slid down the railing, and rushed into his arms.

After her father's short visits ended, Eleanor felt lonely. More sadness was to come. In 1892 her mother went to a hospital for surgery. Shortly after, she became sick and died.

Eight-year-old Eleanor and her brothers went to live with their grandmother Hall. Six months later, Elliot Jr. died of the same illness his mother had.

Eleanor became more shy and fearful. She escaped her feelings by reading letters from her father. "One day I'll leave Grandma's," she thought. "Then it will be just Papa and me."

Elliot wrote to his daughter often. In his letters he said how much he loved her. He described the places they would visit when he got well. He also sent gifts: toys, a puppy, and a pony. Eleanor dreamed of the adventures she and her father would have someday. Then tragedy struck again. Elliot died suddenly after a fall.

Eleanor longed to escape her sad feelings. As she walked in the woods, she imagined her father was still alive. In her daydreams, he was a brave hero. She was the hero's faithful friend.

Although Eleanor's dreams were perfect, her real life was not. She didn't think of herself as pretty or confident. Taller than many girls, Eleanor felt clumsy and awkward. And she did not have many friends.

Her happiest times were the summers she spent at her grandmother's country house. While there, she spent time with family. Every morning Eleanor and her aunt would row across the Hudson River together. Eleanor's uncles taught her to jump horses.

When she wasn't around family, Eleanor recited poetry in her room. She read books, and she wrote her own stories. One tale was about butterflies. Each had a different personality. The first was unhappy with life. **"Pooh!"** it said. **"I'm not going to sit on a daisy always . . . I am going to know a great deal and to see everything."** Another was young and beautiful. **"I've been to at least six dinners and about as many dances in the last week but then it is such fun."**

Eleanor's mother had always wanted her to be educated in Europe. When Eleanor was 15 years old, her grandmother found a school for her. Soon Eleanor was attending a French-speaking boarding school near London.

The school's leader was Mademoiselle Souvestre. Under her care, Eleanor blossomed. Mademoiselle Souvestre knew Eleanor was special. "An excellent child," she wrote. "She is very eager to learn. And she has the warmest heart of anyone I have ever known."

Eleanor's time at school was like no other. For the first time in her life, she enjoyed standing out. She spoke French very well. She learned a lot about the world. She was becoming more confident. She was growing up.

Mademoiselle Souvestre noticed the old-fashioned clothes Eleanor wore. "Why don't you use your money and buy a beautiful dress?" she asked.

Eleanor did. Everyone's eyes were on the well-dressed young woman standing 6 feet (1.8 meters) tall.

Eleanor learned history and studied the arts at school.
She was captain of the field hockey team. Her childhood
fears faded away. She grew to be full of life.

"I feel very happy here," she told a friend. "Many people
love me. And I love them back!"

At the end of three years, it was time to leave school. Eleanor cried as she said goodbye.

Later Mademoiselle Souvestre wrote to her in New York. "I miss you every day of my life."

Eleanor was on her own, and she was ready for big things to come.

Afterword

In 1905 Eleanor married Franklin Roosevelt, her distant cousin. They had known each other their entire lives. They had five children. Eleanor volunteered for the Red Cross in her spare time.

Franklin wanted to be the governor of New York. But in 1921 he found out he had polio. The disease left him unable to move from the waist down. Eleanor urged him to keep running for office. In 1928 he was elected. Six years later he became President of the United States.

As first lady, Eleanor supported civil rights for African Americans, women, and the poor. And she wrote a newspaper column every week. During World War II, she supported women workers. She also helped bring war refugees to the United States.

After Franklin's death in 1945, Eleanor returned to New York. She hosted radio programs and a TV show. She also wrote books and continued her newspaper column. As a U.S. delegate to the United Nations, she helped pass the Universal Human Declaration of Rights. This document defined how people and nations should treat each other. **"I have never felt that anything really mattered but the satisfaction of knowing that you stood for the things in which you believed and had done the very best you could,"** she said.

Eleanor Roosevelt died at age 78 in 1962.

Glossary

accompany—to go somewhere with someone

boarding school—a school where children live during the school year

delegate—a person who is chosen to act for others; a representative

Europe—one of the world's continents

mademoiselle—a title of an unmarried French-speaking woman, like *Miss* in English

recite—to speak out loud from memory

refugee—a person forced to flee his or her home because of natural disaster or war

solemn—serious, not cheerful or smiling

temper—a tendency to suddenly get angry

tragedy—a very sad event

United Nations—a group of countries that works together for peace and security

Read More

Edison, Erin. *Franklin D. Roosevelt*. Presidential Biographies. North Mankato, Minn.: Capstone Press, 2013.

Kimmelman, Leslie. *Hot Dog! Eleanor Roosevelt Throws a Picnic.* Ann Arbor, Mich.: Sleeping Bear Press, 2014.

Lee, Sally. *Eleanor Roosevelt*. First Ladies. Mankato, Minn.: Capstone Press, 2011.

Critical Thinking Questions

1. As a child, Eleanor Roosevelt experienced sorrows and joys. She also had certain advantages and disadvantages. Compare and contrast these sorrows and joys, and advantages and disadvantages.

2. The author says Eleanor's goals as a child were "to love and be loved." Did Eleanor achieve these goals? Explain your answer and use evidence in the text to support it.

3. Construct a time line of Eleanor's life, from the time she was born to the time she passed away.

4. Who were the three most important people in Eleanor's childhood? Use evidence from the text to support your answer.

Index

Internet Sites

Use FactHound to find Internet sites related to this book.

Visit *www.facthound.com*

Just type in this code: 9781515830412 and go.

Super-cool stuff! Check out projects, games and lots more at **www.capstonekids.com**

Other Titles in This Series

WHEN
Amelia Earhart
BUILT A
ROLLER COASTER

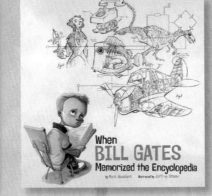

When
BILL GATES
Memorized the Encyclopedia

When
CESAR CHAVEZ
Climbed the Umbrella Tree

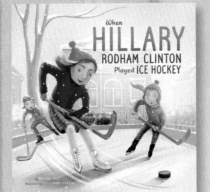

When
HILLARY
RODHAM CLINTON
Played ICE HOCKEY

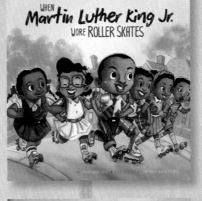

WHEN
Martin Luther King Jr.
WORE ROLLER SKATES

When
NEIL ARMSTRONG
Built a Wind Tunnel

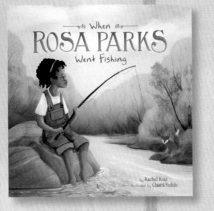

When
ROSA PARKS
Went Fishing

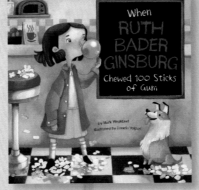

When
RUTH BADER GINSBURG
Chewed 100 Sticks of Gum

WHEN
THOMAS EDISON
FED SOMEONE
WORMS

WHEN
WALT DISNEY
RODE A PIG

When
Wilma Rudolph Played Basketball

Special thanks to our adviser for his advice and expertise:
James N. Druckman
Department of Political Science
Northwestern University
Evanston, Illinois

Editors: Mari Bolte and Shelly Lyons
Designer: Ashlee Suker
Creative Director: Nathan Gassman
Production Specialist: Tori Abraham
The illustrations in this book were created digitally.

Editor's Note: Direct quotations are indicated by **bold** words.

Direct quotations are found on the following pages:
page 6, lines 5-6: Ward, G.C. & Burns, K. *The Roosevelts*. Knopf. NY. 2014. page 47.
page 20, lines 4-7: Wiesen Cook, Blanche. *Eleanor Roosevelt, Volume 1*. Penguin, page 97.
Page 28, lines 17-20: Roosevelt, Eleanor. *My Day*, November 8, 1944.

Picture Window Books are published by Capstone,
1710 Roe Crest Drive, North Mankato, Minnesota 56003
www.mycapstone.com

Copyright © 2019 by Picture Window Books, a Capstone imprint.
All rights reserved. No part of this publication may be reproduced in whole
or in part, or stored in a retrieval system, or transmitted in any form or by
any means, electronic, mechanical, photocopying, recording, or otherwise,
without written permission of the publisher.

Library of Congress Cataloging-in-Publication Data is available
on the Library of Congress website.
ISBN 978-1-5158-3041-2 (library hardcover)
ISBN 978-1-5158-3050-4 (paperback)
ISBN 978-1-5158-3054-2 (eBook PDF)

Printed in the United States   5206